My First ACROSTIC

The East

Edited by Jenni Bannister

First published in Great Britain in 2015 by:

Young**Writers**

Remus House
Coltsfoot Drive
Peterborough
PE2 9BF
Telephone: 01733 890066
Website: www.youngwriters.co.uk

All Rights Reserved
Book Design by Ashley Janson
© Copyright Contributors 2015
ISBN 978-1-78443-575-2

Printed and bound in the UK by BookPrintingUK
Website: www.bookprintinguk.com

FOREWORD

Welcome, Reader!

For Young Writers' latest competition, My First Acrostic, we gave Key Stage 1 children nationwide the challenge of writing an acrostic poem on the topic of their choice.

Poetry is a wonderful way to introduce young children to the idea of rhyme and rhythm and helps learning and development of communication, language and literacy skills. The acrostic form is a great introduction to poetry, giving a simple framework for pupils to structure their thoughts while at the same time allowing more confident writers the freedom to let their imaginations run wild.

Here at Young Writers our aim is to encourage creativity in children and to inspire a love of the written word, so it's great to get such an amazing response, with some absolutely fantastic poems. This made it a tough challenge to pick the winners, so well done to **Aleisha Clarke** who has been chosen as the best poet in this anthology.

Due to the young age of the entrants we have tried to include as many of the poems as possible. By giving these young poets the chance to see their work in print we hope to encourage their love of poetry and give them the confidence to continue with their creative efforts – I look forward to reading more of their poems in the future.

Jenni Bannister
Editorial Manager

CONTENTS

Abbotsmede Primary School, Peterborough
Denis Skudarnov (5) 1

All Saints CE Primary School, Bury St. Edmunds
Freya Dunn (6) 1
Finnian Senior (6) 2
Olivia Scamponi-Grey (6) 2
Nathaniel Gibbs (6) 3
Chloé Haynes (6) 3
Rosie Walters (7) 4
Christian Gibbs (4) 4

Apex Primary School, Ilford
Zahra Amjad (7) 5
Sumaya Bolaon (7) 6
Izma Lucky (6) 7
Yusuf Ali (7) 8
Duaa Akber (7) 9
Nazeeha Kashif (6) 10

Bewick Bridge Community Primary School, Cambridge
Kimani Stephen (6) 10
Gautam Swaminathan (7) 11
Mia Smith (7) 11
Dylan Fairclough (6) 12
Natalie Church (6) 12
Isabel Job (6) 13
Adriano Muzzin (6) 13
Oliver Fisher (6) 14
Hayden Rookes (7) 14
Eliaas-Ijah Ebanks-Blake (7) ... 15
Roice Watts (6) 15

Ashvika Mahant (7) 16
Shaylon Sweeney (7) 16
Aitana Velasco Vega (7) 17
Mason Faustino (6) 17
Maddison Haden (6) 18

Cobholm Primary School, Great Yarmouth
Holly Bryenton-Rochard (6) 18
Sonny Sugeoner (6) 19
Shamia Saunders (7) 19
Lauren Buckland (6) 20
Riley Peter Kingsmith (7) 20
Alf Ellis (7) 21
Demi-Leigh Butterfield (7) 21

Daiglen School, Buckhurst Hill
Marisa Chauhan (7) 22
Jack Kristian Shellard (6) 23
Chloe Zimelstern (7) 24
Mohsen Ameen Malik (6) 25
Milli Harvey (6) 26
Molly Wells (7) 27
Zidaan Jilani (7) 28
Aditi Reddy Ganthi (6) 29
Joseph Matthews (7) 30
Oscar Pearman (7) 31
Georgia Summers (6) 32
Priya Gill (6) 33
Hannah Hussain (7) 34
Samuel Boulton (7) 34
Beau Wise (6) 35

Dell Primary School, Lowestoft
Katie Jones (6) 35
Annabelle Taylor (7) 36
Hope Blizard 37
Cally Smith 38

Sophie May Moore (6)	38
Carmen Akim (6)	39
Sophie Wilson (6)	39
Miriam Louise Holden (7)	40
James Hathaway (6)	40
TJ Godwin (6)	41
Benjamin Littlejohns (6)	41
Mason Gray (7)	42
Charlotte Rainer (5)	42
Marcia Temple (6)	43
Imogen Woods (5)	43
Charlotte Adams (6)	44
Thomas Blowers (7)	44
Miya Rowan-McComb (7)	45
Emily Rogers (7)	45
Harvey Ansdell (6)	46
Thomas Martin (6)	46
Callum Jay Grundy (5)	47
Ashwin Nagendram (6)	47
Alfie Ward (7)	48
Ruby Battershill-Tooke (6)	48
Alexander Hands (7)	49
Gracie-Belle Stokeld (6)	49
Jack Whelan (6)	50
Hayden Earle-Mitchell (7)	50
Phoebe Porter	51
Holly Rowley-White (7)	51
Gabriel Hind (5)	52
Riley Neville (7)	52
Aaron Zhang (6)	53
Emily Neale	53
Lucas Ames (6)	54
Soren Emery (6)	54
Amelie Kinder (6)	55
Lilymae Elliott (7)	55
Abigail Jones (5)	56
Max Fisher (6)	56
Lola Luscher (6)	56
Evie-Rose Fennell (7)	57
Zoe Jade Burgess (5)	57

Forest Academy, Brandon

Phoebe Krieger (5)	57
Tamzin Royal (6)	58
Curtis Powell (6)	58
Anna-Maria Wong (5)	59
Sullivan Topher Goddard (5)	59
Charlie-Jo M Hinton (5)	60
Liliana Wall (6)	60
Oliver Hunt (6)	61
Jayden Lord (5)	61
Samuel Barber (6)	62
Joshua Hayden Clark (6)	62
Jodie Waller (6)	63
Monet Marie James (6)	63
Freya Ann Howlett (6)	64
Holly Mickleburgh (6)	64
Alfie Tokley (5)	65
Milla Clarke (5)	65
Lilly Rissen-Carter (6)	66
Farah Lindsay-Webb (6)	66
Logan Snowdon (5)	67
Luke James Snelling (5)	67
Aira Ozman (6)	68
Ruby Lily Cole-Wilkin (6)	68
Rhys Barton (5)	68
Liam Thomas Burton (6)	69

Great Waldingfield CEVC Primary School, Sudbury

Amelia Morford (7)	69
Theodore Hutchison (5)	70
Ruby Blossom Smith (5)	70
Ethan Chesterman (5)	71
Evelyn Pope (6)	71
Annabelle Hayhow (6)	72
Aleisha Clarke (5)	72
Joshua Jones (5)	73
Annabelle Grace Jane Ward (5)	73
Freddie Kemsley (6)	74
MillieMae Peace Owen (6)	74
Phoebe Goodwin (5)	75
Chloe Newman (6)	75
Lydia Mayes (5)	76
Dylan Carr (7)	76
Esme Violet Louise Turner (7)	77
Chloe Hayton (7)	77
Jake Darren Sparkes (6)	78
Amelia Bartlett (6)	78

Ingoldisthorpe CEVA Primary School, King's Lynn

Charlie Lavvaf (5) 79
Matilda Gray (6) 79
Eleni Marten (6) 80
Rachel Chalmers (6) 80
Charlie Frammingham (5) 81
Millie Hayward (6) 81
Charlie Booth (6) 82
Bradley Ellis (6) 82
Sofia Eaton (5) 83
Poppy Whyman-Naveh (5) 83
Aidan Beagles (7) 84
Holly Ford (6) 84
Evie Wright-Thompson (5) 85
Finn Miller-Neville (6) 85
Harry Hardy (6) 86
Oliver Thaxter (6) 86
Angelina Robinson-Lagopodi (6) 87
Mollie Skerritt (5) 87
Olivia Hammond (7) 88
Max Godwin (5) 88

John Bramston Primary School, Ilford

Gabriella Charlotte Oldham (7) 89
Ruth Sarah Chandy (5) 90
Erin Phippin (6) 90
Abbie Hazelden (5) 91
Isobel Jones (5) 91
Natalie Granese (7) 92
Luke Anthony McManus (6) 92
Matvejs Androsovs (6) 93
Aisha Adebajo-Martinez (7) 93
Connor Joseph Cooper (7) 94
Ariane-Dannielle Forson (6) ... 94
Nia Clairmont (6) 95
Kayah Roznicka (5) 95
Charlotte Ashton (5) 96
Amelie Parr (6) 96
Amy Branch (6) 97
Scarlett Georgina Givens Hunter (6) 97
Marley Stewart (6) 98
Krishna Seeburrun (6) 98

Kishan Shah (5) 99
Amelia Botnari (6) 99
Riley Hunt (6) 100
Alan Oleksiewicz (7) 100
Numaya Polpitye (6) 101
Gram Brazier (5) 101
Daniel Owolabi (6) 102
Sebastian Archire (7) 102
Emma Chikov (7) 103
Hannan Ijaz (7) 103
Rebecca Seville 104
Chloe Lipscombe (6) 104
Parth Joshi (6) 105
Jayden Bahra (6) 105
Noah Demetriades (6) 106
Eliza Holder (7) 106
Ramone Phillips (5) 107

Littlegarth School, Colchester

Milly Down 107
Lauren Valerie Climpson (6) . 108
Isabella Grice (7) 109
Jemima Howard (6) 110
Megan Palmer.......................110
Oliver Pashby (6) 111
Henry Rutland (5) 111
Phoebe Cecilia Racher (6) 112
Henry Staines.......................112
Monty Morgan (7) 113
Krisha Donepudi....................113
Lyla Belshaw (7) 114
Isabella Windridge (5)...........114
Harry Tucker (7).....................115
Isobel Sarah Christey (6).......115
Archie Ball (7) 116
Otis Gee (6) 116
Henrietta Stenning (7)............117
Theodora Langdon (7) 117
Imogen Taylor........................118
Elliott Sadler (7) 118
Samuel Finan 119
Hayden Abishai Swampillai (7)......119
Tait Ferguson (6)................... 120
Alexander Forshaw (5) 120
Tierney Clarke (6) 121
Poppy Down (5).................... 121

Mika Quayyum (5) 122
Angus Strathern (5) 122
Evelyn Cook (6) 123
Samuel Barker 123
Henry John Wilmot Price (6) 124
Theodore Bond Roberts (5) 124
Sebastian Brockman Booth (5) 125
Tilly Sexton (6) 125
Angus Learmont-Adderley (5) 126
Matilda Oliver (5) 126
Charles Langdon (5) 127
Lukas Karlsson (5) 127
Adithi Thayur (6) 128
George Romer-Lee (6) 128
Isaac James Mott (7) 129
Molly Talbot 129
Toby Robert Paul Bryant (7) 130

Roxwell CE Primary School, Chelmsford
Emily Iszatt (7) 130
Charlie Wilson (5) 131
Thomas Porter (5) 131
Olivia Maund (5) 132
Abigail Simpson (7) 132
Hayden Thorneycroft (5) 133
Reece Carter (6) 133
Mya Phillips (6) 134
Aaron Maund (6) 134
Matilda Drakeford (6) 135
Lucy Scott (6) 135
Kaiya Launchbury (5) 136
Nuala Elsie Hedges (7) 136
Liam Wawman (6) 137
Lola Lawrence (5) 137
Daisy Georgina Hedges (7) 138
Luke Carter (5) 138
Scarlett Langley (5) 139

Stukeley Meadows Primary School, Huntingdon
Gauravi Harish 139

THE POEMS

My First Acrostic – The East

Denis

D is for dream, I always like to dream.
E is for easy, I can easily teach lessons.
N is for neat boy, my parents say I am.
I is for ice cream, my favourite delicacy.
S is for sporty, I want to become an Olympic champion.

Denis Skudarnov (5)
Abbotsmede Primary School, Peterborough

Bumblebee

B rilliant black and yellow
U nbelievable sting
M assive hive
B eautiful buzz
L ovely honeycomb
E xciting honey
B usy bees collect nectar
E njoying resting on daisies
E xtraordinary flowers.

Freya Dunn (6)
All Saints CE Primary School, Bury St. Edmunds

Nathanael

N ate is my brother
A nd he's a bit of a rascal
T ea is what he likes to drink
H e is cheeky sometimes
A nd he messes around!
N ate takes off the Lego mini-figures' arms
A nd he chucks them on the floor
E very day he plays with me
L ove him all the much!

Finnian Senior (6)
All Saints CE Primary School, Bury St. Edmunds

Africa

A continent with lots of countries in it; far, far away.
F eeling happy thinking about this amazing place.
R hinos, elephants and other beautiful animals roam the plains.
I n Africa some people live in mud huts.
C hildren of Africa . . . many are poor and have no food or water. I wish I could help them.
A frica, oh Africa, I hope to visit you one day.

Olivia Scamponi-Grey (6)
All Saints CE Primary School, Bury St. Edmunds

Holiday

H ot sunshine
O cean waves, deep, deep
L ove swimming in the ocean
I like playing
D ays are hot
A nd days pass happily
Y es we have a great time.

Nathaniel Gibbs (6)
All Saints CE Primary School, Bury St. Edmunds

Horse

H ow the horse went over the hill
O n a sunny day
R unning, running on the road
S inging at the top of her voice
E veryone gets some hay!

Chloé Haynes (6)
All Saints CE Primary School, Bury St. Edmunds

Jungle Dancing

Z ebras dancing proudly
U nicorns prancing lightly up and down
M onkeys being silly, while
B ees buzz around
A ll the animals dancing happily to the Zumba beat.

Rosie Walters (7)
All Saints CE Primary School, Bury St. Edmunds

Ocean

O ctopus tickling, tickling
C atfish swimming
E lephant seal waiting for his home
A ngel fish swimming deep
N arwhal charging at the ice.

Christian Gibbs (4)
All Saints CE Primary School, Bury St. Edmunds

My First Acrostic – The East

Aegiptosaurus

A mazing to see in a fight
E ager to attack
G iant to stomp on them
I ncredibly strong
P ainful attack
T errifying teeth
O bese and rolling around
S low as a snail
A fraid to fight
U p to no good
R oars like a dragon
U nbelievable hunter
S o epic.

Zahra Amjad (7)
Apex Primary School, Ilford

Austrosaurus

A cts like a predator
U nacceptable predator
S low as a snail
T rots a lot with its feet
R are sight now
O bese and rolling around
S trong in a fight
A fraid to fight
U nbelievably strong
R oars always
U nfair to everyone
S trong, heavy roar!

Sumaya Belaon (7)
Apex Primary School, Ilford

My First Acrostic – The East

Watch Out! Triceratops!

T errifying
R ectifying
I nto the heart of the deadly desert
C an't be beaten
E xpected to pounce on you
R epents
A s tough as a T-rex
T ender, as *if!*
O n operation I need my leaves!
P art of the plant-eater family
S unny days come to it!

Izma Lucky (6)
Apex Primary School, Ilford

Sismosaurus

S o big
I t's more like a giant
S uper
M agnificent
O mnivore
S o tall
A mazing
U nbelievable
R epetitive roar
U gly
S cary.

Yusuf Ali (7)
Apex Primary School, Ilford

My First Acrostic – The East

Diplodocus

D angerous
I nteresting
P icks at anything he likes
L ovely
O dd
D emanding
O range
C luttered
U nacceptable
S creams so loud.

Duaa Akber (7)
Apex Primary School, Ilford

Diplodocus

D iscover
I nvisible
P recious
L ovely
O wn
D isguise
O ffer
C alm
U p
S unny.

Nazeeha Kashif (6)
Apex Primary School, Ilford

Smelly

S tanley the snake loves sheep,
M artin the magpie makes machines,
E liaas eats oranges,
L illy likes lollies,
L ollies are yummy,
Y ucky useful junk.

Kimani Stephen (6)
Bewick Bridge Community Primary School, Cambridge

My First Acrostic – The East

Touch And Taste

T ouching a stone is really fun
O ut of this world to touch moon dust
U nder the moon to touch the stars
C rashing home to touch the Earth!
H ome again, touching the carpet!

T aste a roti from India
A nd a large piece of steak from USA
S nake curry in North India
T aking a ride with sandwiches
E ating and tasting is lots of fun.

Gautam Swaminathan (7)
Bewick Bridge Community Primary School, Cambridge

Smelly

S tinky socks made my bed disgusting,
M y belt was all tucked up,
E lephant stinks because he is big and dusty,
L ettuce is yummy,
L ovely as a spice,
Y ucky lettuce when it is mouldy.

Mia Smith (7)
Bewick Bridge Community Primary School, Cambridge

Smelly

S un smells hot,
M ilk smells cold but sometimes rotten,
E ggs smell hot when they come out of the oven,
L emons smell sour,
L imes smell sour too,
Y ellow bananas smell super fresh like fire.

Dylan Fairclough (6)
Bewick Bridge Community Primary School, Cambridge

Touch

T oday we might go to the farm because it is a lovely day,
O h but Mum, why can't we go now? Okay, okay we can go.
U mm . . . I wonder what animal I should touch first. Got it!
C ome on. Come on. Come ooon! Let's go and touch a foal.
H ow about the horsy? Shall we go to the horsy? Ouch! Ouch! The hedgehog pricked me! It pricked me on the heel!

Natalie Church (6)
Bewick Bridge Community Primary School, Cambridge

My First Acrostic – The East

Smelly

S tinky
M ouldy fish,
E ggs are rotten and really yucky, don't smell them.
L ovely lime, it's okay to smell and it smells
L ike juicy lemons, you should smell them,
Y ummy, smell lime and don't smell yucky things!

Isabel Job (6)
Bewick Bridge Community Primary School, Cambridge

Seeing

S now is icy,
E liaas looks interesting,
E xciting sun in the space,
I went to London and saw Funnybones,
'N o!' said the big skeleton,
'G ood idea,' said the big skeleton.

Adriano Muzzin (6)
Bewick Bridge Community Primary School, Cambridge

Listen

L isten to the ice crack
I gloos melting
S nakes slithering
T rains chuffing
E lephants tooting
N ewspapers scrunching.

Oliver Fisher (6)
Bewick Bridge Community Primary School, Cambridge

Seeing

S ight is amazing bright and dark,
E agles soaring through the air,
E ight stars rising from the sky,
I gloos are icy houses up high,
N ight falls, the sun sets,
G oodbye everyone, see you next time.

Hayden Rookes (7)
Bewick Bridge Community Primary School, Cambridge

Taste

T aste buds are on your tongue,
A pples are nice and ripe
S nakes are slithering but I
T aste a doughnut,
E liaas likes juicy apples.

Eliaas-Ijah Ebanks-Blake (7)
Bewick Bridge Community Primary School, Cambridge

Taste

T astes like a stinking fish in water
A pples are rosy red and juicy
S crummy like a brown cookie
T asty like a cake with chocolate sauce
E ggs taste yummy in a pancake.

Roice Watts (6)
Bewick Bridge Community Primary School, Cambridge

Taste

T asty like a bowl of cream,
A s creamy as an ice cream,
S izzling sausages in my mouth,
T winkly types of lemon (sour as salt),
E veryone loves creamy chocolate.

Ashvika Mahant (7)
Bewick Bridge Community Primary School, Cambridge

Taste

T asty crisps,
A s yummy as a fish,
S o cool and crunchy,
T astes salty,
E very day I eat my crisps.

Shaylon Sweeney (7)
Bewick Bridge Community Primary School, Cambridge

My First Acrostic – The East

Taste

T offee is as chewy as chewing gum,
A red apple is as crunchy as a crisp
S peeding down my throat. Coca-Cola is very
T angy but
E veryone loves creamy chocolate.

Aitana Velasco Vega (7)
Bewick Bridge Community Primary School, Cambridge

Taste

T oys in my mouth
A pples fighting aliens,
S neaky snakes bite your arm off,
T asty cakes could be poisonous,
E ating is dangerous!

Mason Faustino (6)
Bewick Bridge Community Primary School, Cambridge

Tasty

T asty toy in my sister's mouth
A liens attacked my sister's apple,
S lippery snakes like smelly slippers
T immy the dog likes licking shoes
Y ucky pasta like a stinky fish.

Maddison Haden (6)
Bewick Bridge Community Primary School, Cambridge

Plants

P lants grow in slow motion every day,
L ilies are very white
A nts are so tiny
N eat grow the roses and roses growing
T horns are hard
S un helps the flowers grow.

Holly Bryenton-Rochard (6)
Cobholm Primary School, Great Yarmouth

My First Acrostic – The East

Plants

P retty flowers.
L ilies are beautiful
A nts eat plants.
N ettles are as sharp as a knife.
T errifying stinging nettles are sharp.
S cented flowers.

Sonny Sugeoner (6)
Cobholm Primary School, Great Yarmouth

Plants

P lants grow in the sun
L ots of them grow in the day
A flower grows in the day
N ow they need the sun
T he flowers need lots of water
S un and rain and rain again.

Shamia Saunders (7)
Cobholm Primary School, Great Yarmouth

Plants

P lants grow at the speed of a snail,
L ayers flutter down from the sky
A plant swaying through the wind
N uts are very tasty
T V has lots of programmes of
S limy slugs slithering over the plants.

Lauren Buckland (6)
Cobholm Primary School, Great Yarmouth

Plants

P lants grow like a slug, like a snail.
L eaves drop slowly off the trees.
A pples fall off the tree when they have finished growing.
N ext grow the roses, like a slow sludge.
T V shows the roses in spring,
S lowly grow the flowers.

Riley Peter Kingsmith (7)
Cobholm Primary School, Great Yarmouth

My First Acrostic – The East

Plants

P lants grow slowly
L ike petals growing in the dark
A piece of pollen floats everywhere
N ettles sting
T he yellow pollen falls on another flower
S o the seed grows.

Alf Ellis (7)
Cobholm Primary School, Great Yarmouth

Demi

D emi is a very beautiful name,
E ducated and energetic,
M arvellous runner,
I ndependent learner.

Demi-Leigh Butterfield (7)
Cobholm Primary School, Great Yarmouth

Marisa Chauhan

My name is Marisa Chauhan
A ccurate at maths
R esponsible for ideas
I maginative in art
S uper at lots of things
A dored by my mummy's friends and family

C alm wherever I go
H indi is my religion
A ctive at school
U nselfish to everyone
H ealthy because I love salad
A ctor because I do drama
N ice to everyone.

Marisa Chauhan (7)
Daiglen School, Buckhurst Hill

My First Acrostic – The East

All About Me

A lways like to hang out with my friends
L ove my Mummy, Daddy, Adam and Jamie
L ove also my cousins Imi and Ami

A t home always have a lot of fun
B est friends are called Sam and Joe
O n Thursday I go to Kung-Fu Kickboxing and Chinese stick work
U nderstand English and a bit of Spanish
T uesday I go swimming

M y middle name is Kristian
E njoy going to music lessons with Darcey my friend.

Jack Kristian Shellard (6)
Daiglen School, Buckhurst Hill

All About Me

A lways love homework and school
L ove to read
L ove my mum and dad

A lways like my teddies
B rother is at uni and I miss him
O utstanding teachers!
U ncle Marc came back from America
T alented at singing

M albec, my dog, is crazy!
E ngland is the only country I've lived in.

Chloe Zimelstern (7)
Daiglen School, Buckhurst Hill

All About Me

A lways wanted a cat
L ove swimming in the sea
L ike fruit and vegetables

A lways enjoy Isa coming round
B ad dreams can be scary
O range is my brother's favourite colour
U nderstand and know Urdu and English
T he football on TV is my favourite

M y family love reading books
E veryone misses Dad when he's away.

Mohsen Ameen Malik (6)
Daiglen School, Buckhurst Hill

All About Me

A mazing at gymnastics
L oud in the playground
L ove my family

A lways playing with my dog
B aking is my favourite hobby
O n the ice I like to skate
U nderstand Spanish, the language
T wo of my friends are called George and Hannah

M y dog is called Buddy
E ating little bits of sweets makes me go crazy.

Milli Harvey (6)
Daiglen School, Buckhurst Hill

My First Acrostic – The East

All About Me

A lways like to spend time with my cousin
L anguages I speak are English, German and Spanish
L ove cuddling Mum

A lways like to play
B est friend is Darcey
O ften I go to ballet
U nbelievable at cartwheels
T ea is lovely to drink

M y dad is Irish
E rin is my middle name.

Molly Wells (7)
Daiglen School, Buckhurst Hill

All About Me

A lways like playing Skylanders Trap Team
L ove my little cousins
L ike my friends Beau and Zachary

A lways playing with my favourite, Skylander Blackout
B owling with my friends
O ctopus and whale facts
U SA is my favourite country
T alking English and American

M aking paper planes
E mailing my cousins on their birthdays.

Zidaan Jilani (7)
Daiglen School, Buckhurst Hill

My First Acrostic – The East

All About Me

A lways love spending time with my pet fish
L ove Mum and Dad
L ate for school sometimes

A diti is my name
B aking cakes is my favourite hobby
O nly know how to speak Spanish, English and Telugu
U mbrellas keep the rain away from me
T alented at playing piano

M y favourite toy is my toy zoomer
E njoy playing with my pet fish.

Aditi Reddy Ganthi (6)
Daiglen School, Buckhurst Hill

All About Me

A lways love roller coasters
L ove Mummy and Daddy
L ate for school on Fridays!
A ll the time I'm happy
B rother breaks my stuff
O nly speak Spanish and English
U ncle Terry is really fun
T V is awesome
M eat is my favourite food
E veryone is my friend.

Joseph Matthews (7)
Daiglen School, Buckhurst Hill

My First Acrostic – The East

All About Me

A lways like to stroke my cat
L ike to cuddle my mum
L ike to watch TV

A lways like presents to open
B alls are hard to kick
O ctopi are gross
U sed to go to karate lessons
T ea is the grossest drink in the world

M eat is good for you
E ggs are nice.

Oscar Pearman (7)
Daiglen School, Buckhurst Hill

All About Me

A nnabell is my mummy's name
L ove Mummy and Daddy
L ove Frankie and Molly

A lways have fun at home
B ear is my best and loveliest toy
O livia is my best friend and she goes to a different school
U nderstand English and a bit of Spanish
T eddy is called Teddy

M ummy is whom I love so much
E njoy going to the park.

Georgia Summers (6)
Daiglen School, Buckhurst Hill

All About Me

A nother rabbit for my bunny Dais,y I would like!
L ibby is my neighbour, she is very kind.
L ove a bigger bedroom if my parents agree!

A llowed to wear make-up never!
B aking is what I like to do.
O range is my favourite colour.
U nderstand Punjabi, English, Italian, French and Spanish.
T anisha is my best friend.

M y grandparents are very funny.
E njoy playing with my little brother.

Priya Gill (6)
Daiglen School, Buckhurst Hill

All About Me

A mazing, I am amazing at running
L ove my family
L amborghinis are one of my favourite cars

A nna, my name is Hannah and it rhymes with Anna
B eautiful flowers smell nice
O ranges are my favourite fruit
U nderstand Arabic a little
T ime to party!

M y friends are called Milli and Georgia
E njoy watching The Boxtrolls.

Hannah Hussain (7)
Daiglen School, Buckhurst Hill

Samuel

S am is my name and I'm the boss of the Purple Hand Gang. I
A m imaginative and
M arvellous at being a scientist. I'm
U nbelievably good at dancing. I like boiled
E ggs with beans, bacon and toast. I like to
L ick lollipops until my tongue turns multi-coloured like a rainbow.

Samuel Boulton (7)
Daiglen School, Buckhurst Hill

My First Acrostic – The East

All About Me

B is for beautiful
E is for Easter, I like chocolate eggs
A is for amazing at singing
U is for uncle, my favourite uncle
W is for wave which I like to do
I is for ice which I like to touch
S is for swamp which is wet and smelly
E is for eagles which I like to watch flying.

Beau Wise (6)
Daiglen School, Buckhurst Hill

Snowflake

S nowy in the sky
N ot that cold
O n the rooftops
W ith magic
F looded with snow
L ovely as a pillow
A mazing as ever
K ind, calm and still
E ven settling.

Katie Jones (6)
Dell Primary School, Lowestoft

My Best Friend

M addison is my best friend
Y ellow is her favourite colour

B eautiful she is and her smile never fades
E specially if we are having fun together
S o I think she's number one!
T o her I write to tell her good news, she can come to my house.

'F antastic!' she shouts. 'I'm going to her house!'
R eady in the car her mum drives her to mine
I am the most excited, 'Yay!'
E xcept time flies fast and soon she goes away,
N o doubt that she will tell me one
D ay that I will come to hers.

Annabelle Taylor (7)
Dell Primary School, Lowestoft

Untitled

M y family is nice
U mbrellas keep you dry
M ums are good

H ugs are nice
O ranges are yummy
P eople love to squeeze me
E mma is my auntie

F amily makes me happy
A cuddle in the morning
M y mummy makes me smile
I love my family
L ove is what makes a happy family
Y ou make me smile too.

Hope Blizard
Dell Primary School, Lowestoft

Cally Smith

C olouring
A pples
L ollipops
L oom-bands
Y ellow

S inging
M um
I ce cream
T V
H air.

Cally Smith
Dell Primary School, Lowestoft

Snowing

S uddenly it's white everywhere
N ow we need to find our gloves
O utside we go!
W hen building a snowman
I cy cold friends – brrr
N ow it's time to come in
G etting warm by the fire.

Sophie May Moore (6)
Dell Primary School, Lowestoft

Ferrets

F errets are fun
E ggs are ferrets' favourite treats
R olling in the dirt is a ferret's thing
R acing through tunnels, dancing round bends, that's why ferrets are my friends
E scaping through holes just has to be done, that's why ferrets are so much fun
T hieving and stashing is a ferret's game, so if you leave your valuables out, you are to blame
S mell very stinky but I don't care, I love ferrets, so there!

Carmen Akim (6)
Dell Primary School, Lowestoft

Dancing

D ancing is the best
A cross the floor we move
N ever to be late, we try
C oncentrating on the teacher's words
I n and out we point our toes
N early time to put on a show
G entle arms move up and down.

Sophie Wilson (6)
Dell Primary School, Lowestoft

Wintertime

W inter is cold
I ce is too
N oses are red
T rees are like new
E ars get all achy
R ight in my head
T ime for hot choccy
I t's time for my bed
M ornings are frosty, evenings are dark
E ven the poor dogs are starting to bark.

Miriam Louise Holden (7)
Dell Primary School, Lowestoft

Snowman

S nowflakes fall down
N ot long to wait now
O h I can't wait
W inter is so great
M aking snowmen in the snow
A choo! Wrap up warm
N ow my snowman is done.

James Hathaway (6)
Dell Primary School, Lowestoft

Ted Sonic

T ed is my best teddy
E very day I play with him
D on't forget to play with him

S onic is fast
O n the telly I watch him
N ow I have him I can play with him
I 've got him in teddy version
C oolest teddy!

TJ Godwin (6)
Dell Primary School, Lowestoft

Legoland

L ego is fun to build with
E very Lego block is a different shape and size
G ood times at Legoland
O bjects everywhere are made of Lego
L and of the Vikings
A dventure land
N ight-time in the hotel
D one at Legoland, time to go home.

Benjamin Littlejohns (6)
Dell Primary School, Lowestoft

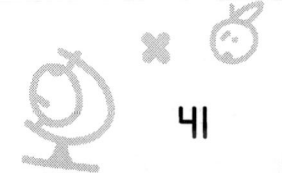

Diabetes

D iagnosed with Type 1 diabetes
I njecting insulin to keep me well
A t the hospital I had to stay
B rave I have to be
E ating healthy food
T eaching people how to help me
E very meal I need to take my medicine
S upport is given by lots of people.

Mason Gray (7)
Dell Primary School, Lowestoft

Seahorse

S eahorse is special to me, I love him to bits
E very night I like to sleep with him
A very special toy is special to everybody
H e is fluffy and very cuddly and he likes big hugs
O range fins, a blue body and yellow belly
R eady to sing when I squeeze his tummy
S weet music that helps me go to sleep
E very night I give him a kiss and say goodnight.

Charlotte Rainer (5)
Dell Primary School, Lowestoft

My First Acrostic – The East

Earmuffs

E xciting new earmuffs
A rriving from Argos
R apidly I open the box
M um says be careful
U h-oh, I will cut my hand
F ind a plaster
F ine again
S uper warm ears.

Marcia Temple (6)
Dell Primary School, Lowestoft

Sausages

S ausage is my favourite food
A s I eat them lots
U sually I eat them with chips
S ome sausages I eat cold
A nd some I like hot
G ravy goes well with sausages
E gg is quite nice too
S ausage is my favourite food, how about you?

Imogen Woods (5)
Dell Primary School, Lowestoft

Dancing

D ancing is my favourite thing to do
A crobatics is where I learn to do the splits
N ight-time is when I dream about dancing
C harlotte taps and everybody claps
I love to dance
N ursery is when I started to dance
G racefully and elegantly I move.

Charlotte Adams (6)
Dell Primary School, Lowestoft

Fishing

F ishing is awesome
I t is my favourite thing to do
S trike when the float goes underwater
H ooks are used to catch fish
I t's good to go fishing in the summer
N ibble is what fishes do to the maggots
G o home after catching lots of fish.

Thomas Blowers (7)
Dell Primary School, Lowestoft

My First Acrostic – The East

Snowman

S now is freezing cold
N ot like the sun.
O ver the hills,
W hite snow glistens
M agical winter,
A lovely time of year.
N ever leave the house without your warm gear.

Miya Rowan-McComb (7)
Dell Primary School, Lowestoft

Kittens

K ittens are cute
I n the park or anywhere
T hey're so fluffy
T ummy to head
E very day
N ot a flea on her fur
S apphire the cat does though!

Emily Rogers (7)
Dell Primary School, Lowestoft

Beavers

B eavers try their best
E ach and every day
A nywhere, any place
V ery hard work
E veryone takes part
R oyal Navy flag
S ea Scouts are the best.

Harvey Ansdell (6)
Dell Primary School, Lowestoft

Dragon

D ragons are dangerous
R eptiles that fly
A lmost all dragons can breathe fire
G liding through the sky
O ctopus is one of their favourite treats
N ight Fury is a super dragon.

Thomas Martin (6)
Dell Primary School, Lowestoft

Batman

B est hero in the whole world
A rch-enemies beware!
T he Joker doesn't stand a chance
M any times he's tried
A ll of which he's failed
N o man can defeat him.

Callum Jay Grundy (5)
Dell Primary School, Lowestoft

Summer

S ummer is sunny
U pset when summer is over
M y birthday is in summer
M elting ice cream is yummy
E veryone loves summer
R acing outside and having fun.

Ashwin Nagendram (6)
Dell Primary School, Lowestoft

Footie!

F ootball, football can make you fit
O ffside rule is confusing a little bit
O bviously scoring is the best part
T eamwork and training is where you start
I cy pitches are not so fun
E veryone claps when you've won.

Alfie Ward (7)
Dell Primary School, Lowestoft

Rabbit

R abbits are really good pets
A twitching nose and bold eyes.
B ouncing around is what they love.
B ig teeth for chomping carrots,
I n the wild or in a hutch.
T iny or big, I love them so much.

Ruby Battershill-Tooke (6)
Dell Primary School, Lowestoft

My First Acrostic – The East

Nissan

N ice Nissan drives through Manchester
I would like a Nissan
S imon is my dad
S imon likes Nissans too
A GTR is my favourite
N issans are cool.

Alexander Hands (7)
Dell Primary School, Lowestoft

Gracie

G is for grass which I walk on every day
R is for red, which is the colour of my school coat
A is for apple which I love to eat
C is for cupboard, which I put my toys in
I is for interesting, which I always am
E is for elephant, which I like to ride on.

Gracie-Belle Stokeld (6)
Dell Primary School, Lowestoft

Batman

B ruce Wayne is my real name
A lfred is my butler
T he Joker is my enemy
M artian Manhunter is my space friend
A wesome bat skills is what I have
N ever give up saving the world.

Jack Whelan (6)
Dell Primary School, Lowestoft

Hayden

H is for having fun with my friends
A is for always being polite
Y is for young and fast at running
D is for doing good in class
E is for enjoying games
N is for never being sad.

Hayden Earle-Mitchell (7)
Dell Primary School, Lowestoft

My First Acrostic – The East

Phoebe

P is for pretty, my mum calls me
H is for as happy as can be
O is for outspoken, my daddy tells me
E is for excellent at being a big sister
B is for being brilliant at my rainbow cubes
E is for entertaining, my nanny says.

Phoebe Porter
Dell Primary School, Lowestoft

Holly

H is for Holly, a bush with red berries
O is for outside where I like to play
L is for Lily, a flower so pretty, just like my sister
L is for love, I love my family and doing fun things
Y is for year, my first year living in England.

Holly Rowley-White (7)
Dell Primary School, Lowestoft

Horse

H orses jump hurdles
O n a racecourse
R acing is fun
S addles are for sitting on
E veryone cheers them on.

Gabriel Hind (5)
Dell Primary School, Lowestoft

Riley

R is for rhino, they always bat
I is for igloo, this is where penguins live
L is for lions, crashing through the jungle
E is for elephants, they stomp, stomp, stomp
Y is for Yarmouth, a town with lots of shops.

Riley Neville (7)
Dell Primary School, Lowestoft

My First Acrostic – The East

Aaron

A is for ace, which my mum says I am
A is for always, I always love my dad
R is for rat, which is my year of birth
O is for orange, which is juicy and sweet
N is for new which starts the year again.

Aaron Zhang (6)
Dell Primary School, Lowestoft

Emily

E is for excited, I am happy
M is for my mum, she is the best
I is for I can nearly do the splits
L is for love because I love my family
Y is for yo-yo, my mum says I always bounce around.

Emily Neale
Dell Primary School, Lowestoft

Lucas

L is for loveable
U is for unique
C is for clown
A is for awesome
S is for silly.

Lucas Ames (6)
Dell Primary School, Lowestoft

Soren

S now falling on my head
O h, it's white and fluffy
R oofs shining with snow
E very child is happy
N ever go away snow!

Soren Emery (6)
Dell Primary School, Lowestoft

My First Acrostic – The East

James

J ames is my brother
A nd we love each other
M y brother is a monster
E specially when he makes me jump
S ometimes he makes me scream!

Amelie Kinder (6)
Dell Primary School, Lowestoft

Jane

J is for jam you spread on your bread
A is for apple, rosy red
N is for numbers you count in your head
E is for evening when you go to bed.

Lilymae Elliott (7)
Dell Primary School, Lowestoft

Snow

S nowmen are fun to build
N ature brings us snow
O ooh! is the sound I make when I go sledging
W inter is when snow comes.

Abigail Jones (5)
Dell Primary School, Lowestoft

Owls

O wls searching for their prey
W ings flapping through the sky
L ooking all around, as only they can do
S aying 'Twit' and waiting for a 'Twoo'.

Max Fisher (6)
Dell Primary School, Lowestoft

Lola

L is for love, I love my family
O is for Olaf, he is in my favourite film
L is for Luscher, that is my surname
A is for Anabell, she is my favourite baby doll.

Lola Luscher (6)
Dell Primary School, Lowestoft

My First Acrostic – The East

Cat

C ats are cuddly and I love to cuddle my cat
A is for adventurous. Me and my cat go on lots
T is for tame and he likes to be stroked by people.

Evie-Rose Fennell (7)
Dell Primary School, Lowestoft

Zoe

Z is for zebra, it has black and white stripes
O is for octopus, they have eight legs
E is for elephant, they have long trunks.

Zoe Jade Burgess (5)
Dell Primary School, Lowestoft

Phoebe

P is for pineapple because I like pineapples
H is for help because people need help
O is for oak because that is my class
E is for eggs because I like eggs
B is for ballet because I'm good
E is for elephant because they're my favourite.

Phoebe Krieger (5)
Forest Academy, Brandon

Tamzin Royal

T is for terrible
A is for asthma because kids have it
M is for monkey because I am one
Z is for zoo because zebras live there
I is for ice because it's icy
N is for natural because I'm a natural

R is for rich because a king and queen are rich
O is for October because it's my birthday
Y is for my yo-yo because I'm not good at them
A is for acting because I'm good at acting
L is for Lego because I can make stuff.

Tamzin Royal (6)
Forest Academy, Brandon

Curtis

C is for clever people
U is for useful and good
R is for really rich
T, I am on time
I am clever and interesting
S is for sensitive.

Curtis Powell (6)
Forest Academy, Brandon

My First Acrostic – The East

Anna-Maria

A is for apple because I like apples
N is for nice knitting because I knit every day
N is for Nanny because I love Nanny
A is for alligator because they're funny

M is for monster because they scare me
A is for auntie because I like my auntie
R is for rubber because I love rubbers
I is for igloo, because I like igloos
A is for Amber because she is my friend.

Anna-Maria Wong (5)
Forest Academy, Brandon

Sullivan

S is for super at maths
U is for untidy
L is for love
L is for lovely
I is for impressive
V is for a van
A is for ace
N is for nice.

Sullivan Topher Goddard (5)
Forest Academy, Brandon

Charlie-Jo

C is for cat because I like cats
H is for hat because I keep my head covered
A is for ant
R is for red
L is for leg
I is for igloo
E is for egg

J is for jaguar
O is for outside.

Charlie-Jo M Hinton (5)
Forest Academy, Brandon

Liliana

L is for loveable
I is for incredible
L is for lucky
I is for interesting
A is for active
N is for nice and lovely
A is for amazing.

Liliana Wall (6)
Forest Academy, Brandon

My First Acrostic – The East

Oliver

O is for Oliver is amazing
L is for lovely and cute
I is for incredible
V is for very brave
E is for endearing
R is for reading.

Oliver Hunt (6)
Forest Academy, Brandon

Jayden

J is for jumping on the trampoline
A is for apple eating
Y is for yo-yo
D is for dinosaur
E is for elephant
N is for night.

Jayden Lord (5)
Forest Academy, Brandon

Samuel

S is for smile
A is for amazing
M is for maths
U is for upstairs
E is for excellent
L , I like my work.

Samuel Barber (6)
Forest Academy, Brandon

Joshua

J is for Joshua
O is for own
S is for Santa
H is for help
U is for untie
A is for ambitious.

Joshua Hayden Clark (6)
Forest Academy, Brandon

My First Acrostic – The East

Jodie

J is for jolly with people
O is for octopus, I am as happy as an octopus
D , I am delightful
I am incredible
E is for excellent, I am excellent at dancing.

Jodie Waller (6)
Forest Academy, Brandon

Monet

M is for monster because I like them
O is for oranges because I like eating them
N is for nails because I have nails
E is for elephant because elephants are cute and funny
T is for a cup of tea.

Monet Marie James (6)
Forest Academy, Brandon

Freya

F is for fantastic because I am kind
R is for respectful because I show respect
E is for excellent because I am pretty
Y is for six years old
A is for amazing and kind.

Freya Ann Howlett (6)
Forest Academy, Brandon

Untitled

H is happy and nice
O is opening
L is really loving
L is so lovely
Y is for you are a winner.

Holly Mickleburgh (6)
Forest Academy, Brandon

My First Acrostic – The East

Alfie

A is for Alfie
L is for lucky
F is for family
I is for inviting people to play
E is for exciting.

Alfie Tokley (5)
Forest Academy, Brandon

Milla

M is for meetings
I is for ice
L is for lollipop
L is for Lipsyl
A is for apple.

Milla Clarke (5)
Forest Academy, Brandon

Lilly

L is for Lego because it's good and you can build it
I is for igloos because it's cold
L is for lights because they make it bright
L is for lights because they help you see
Y is for you because you can do it.

Lilly Rissen-Carter (6)
Forest Academy, Brandon

Farah

F is for fabulous
A is for amazing
R is for respect
A is for active
H is for happy and nice.

Farah Lindsay-Webb (6)
Forest Academy, Brandon

My First Acrostic – The East

Logan

L is for Lego
O is for orange
G is for giant
A is for apple
N is for night.

Logan Snowdon (5)
Forest Academy, Brandon

Luke

L is for light, it's shining in the sky
U is for umbrella
K is for kit when I go to football
E is for egg.

Luke James Snelling (5)
Forest Academy, Brandon

Aira

A is for amazing
I is for ice cream
R is for rug
A is for apple.

Aira Ozman (6)
Forest Academy, Brandon

Ruby

R is for red because it's my favourite colour
U is for umbrella because it's for playing in the rain
B is for bunny because they are cute
Y is for yoghurt.

Ruby Lily Cole-Wilkin (6)
Forest Academy, Brandon

Rhys

R is for reading to my sister
H is for happy
Y is for young
S is for super.

Rhys Barton (5)
Forest Academy, Brandon

My First Acrostic – The East

Liam

L is for Liam
I is for ice cream
A is for amazing
M is for Minecraft.

Liam Thomas Burton (6)
Forest Academy, Brandon

Disneyland Was Amazing!

D isney is my favourite
I t's a magical place
S now White was so beautiful
N o time to be bored
E verybody is always happy
Y oung and old enjoy the fun
L ots of rides to go on
A ll the princesses were there
N ow I want to go back
D isneyland was amazing!

Amelia Morford (7)
Great Waldingfield CEVC Primary School, Sudbury

Spider-Man

S is for Spider-Man
P is for Peter Parker, his name
I is for I play Spider-Man games
D is for danger as he protects us
E is for elastic web
R is for red and blue, his costume
M is for Mary Jane, his friend
A is for Aunt May
N is for New York, his home he keeps safe.

Theodore Hutchison (5)
Great Waldingfield CEVC Primary School, Sudbury

Grandads

G randads are the best
R eady to play
A lways there if I fall
N anny's best friend
D oing funny tricks
A lways making me laugh
D ouble the fun, my special Grandad and my magic Gand
S pecial people who I love.

Ruby Blossom Smith (5)
Great Waldingfield CEVC Primary School, Sudbury

Transport

T rucks and tanks are so much fun
R oads and railways are exciting too
A eroplanes are super speedy
N aughty drivers go too fast
S team trains have old carriages
P orts are busy with boats and ferries
O ld London buses are dusty
R ed and blue tractors are cool
T ube trains travel underground.

Ethan Chesterman (5)
Great Waldingfield CEVC Primary School, Sudbury

Summer

S ummer sunshine is sparkling like a jewel in the sky
U mbrellas are sometimes needed to shade me from the dazzling sun
M y favourite thing to cool me down is sloppy strawberry ice cream
M usic plays into our garden while I dance in the warm sun
E ating tasty burgers that Daddy has cooked on the barbecue
R unning around our camper van on a chirpy campsite.

Evelyn Pope (6)
Great Waldingfield CEVC Primary School, Sudbury

Whippet

While I was at my nanny's my mum and dad picked up a puppy
H is name is Jenson Button Hayhow
I was very excited when I saw him for the first time
P eople say he is very skinny but to me he is perfect
P ractising tricks is lots of fun
E very winter when it snows he goes bonkers
T reats for dogs are very yummy too.

Annabelle Hayhow (6)
Great Waldingfield CEVC Primary School, Sudbury

Mermaids

M ore beautiful than anyone I've ever seen
E very night you're in my dream
R eaching out across the sea
M ermaid you're so kind to me
A lways there when I need a hand
I n the sea or on the land
D reaming of you here with me
S weet and beautiful as can be.

Aleisha Clarke (5)
Great Waldingfield CEVC Primary School, Sudbury

Wilbur

Wilbur is very soft
 I like Wilbur because he is very fluffy
 L ucky Winnie had a friend called Wilbur
 B e careful Winnie might put a spell on you
 U p in the sky you can see Winnie and Wilbur flying in their rocket
 R emember black cats can be lucky.

Joshua Jones (5)
Great Waldingfield CEVC Primary School, Sudbury

Summer

S unflowers grow tall in summer
 U p in the blue sky there are stripy bees, fluttering butterflies and spotty ladybirds
 M mm, yummy vanilla ice cream at the beach
 M onkeys and turtles munching their food at the zoo
 E xcited when we play on holiday
 R unning around in the park with some friends.

Annabelle Grace Jane Ward (5)
Great Waldingfield CEVC Primary School, Sudbury

Freddie

F is for football, I like scoring goals
R is for running fast to school
E is for eating healthy food
D is for dancing to funny music
D is for drinking milk
I is for inviting my friends for tea
E is for exercising every day.

Freddie Kemsley (6)
Great Waldingfield CEVC Primary School, Sudbury

Barbie

B arbie has a girl called Skipper
A dog loves water like a cow
R abbit loves eggs like an apple
B lack dog hiding amongst the shadows
I nk drops like a black bubbling cauldron
E ric the horse galloping and banging loudly.

MillieMae Peace Owen (6)
Great Waldingfield CEVC Primary School, Sudbury

Winter

W inter is very cold
 I t sometimes snows
 N ighttime comes earlier
 T rees don't have any leaves
 E veryone wears hats and gloves
 R ed noses all around.

Phoebe Goodwin (5)
Great Waldingfield CEVC Primary School, Sudbury

Winter

W arm hot chocolate for us to drink
 I ce crystals shimmering, *clink, clink, clink*
 N eatly decorated Christmas trees
 T his season is the best to me
 E verlasting love shown at this time of year
 R oaring log fires make us cheer.

Chloe Newman (6)
Great Waldingfield CEVC Primary School, Sudbury

Summer

S easide trips are always fun
U mbrellas up to protect us from the sun
M y holiday was amazing at the beach
M y dad built me a huge sandcastle
E very day I have an ice cream
R eally cold sea.

Lydia Mayes (5)
Great Waldingfield CEVC Primary School, Sudbury

Autumn

A is for August, that is the end of summer
U is for umbrella, you will need one
T is for tractors ready to cut crops
U is under the lower sun
M is mud for me to splash in
N is for the nice time of year.

Dylan Carr (7)
Great Waldingfield CEVC Primary School, Sudbury

My First Acrostic – The East

Winnie

Winnie has a red, pointy nose
I n her castle it is pitch black
N ow is her time in her play
'No,' she said, 'I don't want to do the play'
I n her world she has a cat called Wilbur
E very day she does spells.

Esme Violet Louise Turner (7)
Great Waldingfield CEVC Primary School, Sudbury

Winter

Warm coats
I cy cars
N ever hot
T winkly lights
E specially freezing
R eally cold.

Chloe Hayton (7)
Great Waldingfield CEVC Primary School, Sudbury

Winter

W inter is windy and cold
I cy ground that crunches under my feet
N ice, warm baths to warm me up
T oasting marshmallows by the fire
E njoying playing in the snow
R esting in blankets watching films.

Jake Darren Sparkes (6)
Great Waldingfield CEVC Primary School, Sudbury

Party

P retty pink is the colour of my birthday dress
A mazing time I am going to have with my friends
R ainbow Fun is where the party is at
T ea and cake we are going to eat
Y elling and screaming, running about too.

Amelia Bartlett (6)
Great Waldingfield CEVC Primary School, Sudbury

My First Acrostic – The East

Birds

B irds are colourful
I n the sky
R ed birds
D aring birds can fly
S o beautiful.

Charlie Lavvaf (5)
Ingoldisthorpe CEVA Primary School, King's Lynn

Birds

B irds are darting
I like birds
R oaming birds
D arting birds
S ome birds are colourful.

Matilda Gray (6)
Ingoldisthorpe CEVA Primary School, King's Lynn

Birds

B irds flying
I nto the sky
R oaming birds
D arting birds
S wooping seagulls.

Eleni Marten (6)
Ingoldisthorpe CEVA Primary School, King's Lynn

Birds

B irds fly up in the sky nice and high
I nto the sky they go
R oaming through the sky
D arting as they go
S eagulls fly at the sea, they like it there.

Rachel Chalmers (6)
Ingoldisthorpe CEVA Primary School, King's Lynn

My First Acrostic – The East

Birds

B irds can fly
I n the beautiful sky
R obins are my favourite birds
D ashing by
S o now all the birds are tired.

Charlie Frammingham (5)
Ingoldisthorpe CEVA Primary School, King's Lynn

Birds

B irds can fly good
I nto the sky
R ain is trouble for birds
D ancing birds flap their wings
S ilently they fly.

Millie Hayward (6)
Ingoldisthorpe CEVA Primary School, King's Lynn

Birds

B irds make nests
I saw a bird
R ight in the sky
D arting
S eagulls.

Charlie Booth (6)
Ingoldisthorpe CEVA Primary School, King's Lynn

Birds

B irds go everywhere
I n-between the trees they go
R ushing round and round
D arting down to get their food
S inging as they go.

Bradley Ellis (6)
Ingoldisthorpe CEVA Primary School, King's Lynn

Birds

B irds make nests
I saw a bird
R aven
D ashing
S himmer.

Sofia Eaton (5)
Ingoldisthorpe CEVA Primary School, King's Lynn

Birds

B irds in summer, they build nests
I n the winter they rest
R un around in the sky
D inner on the ground
S un on their backs.

Poppy Whyman-Naveh (5)
Ingoldisthorpe CEVA Primary School, King's Lynn

Birds

B irds can fly in the sky
I nto the icy wind
R obins have orange on their chest
D ucks have babies
S himmer.

Aidan Beagles (7)
Ingoldisthorpe CEVA Primary School, King's Lynn

Birds

B irds eat bird seed
I have seen birds make nests
R oaming birds can fly
D oves are peaceful
S wallows fly in the sky.

Holly Ford (6)
Ingoldisthorpe CEVA Primary School, King's Lynn

Birds

B irds make nests to lay eggs
I n summer it is warm
R eally like worms
D arting in the sky
S eagulls flying around.

Evie Wright-Thompson (5)
Ingoldisthorpe CEVA Primary School, King's Lynn

Birds

B irds are amusing because they are colourful
I saw a blackbird
R obins fly really fast
D arting birds are amazing
S ome birds are epic.

Finn Miller-Neville (6)
Ingoldisthorpe CEVA Primary School, King's Lynn

Birds

B irds have babies
I n warm nests
R obins have different colours
D arting, they can fly
S o birds can eat sandwiches.

Harry Hardy (6)
Ingoldisthorpe CEVA Primary School, King's Lynn

Birds

B irds flying high
I nto the sky
R oaming round and round
D arting round and out
S hooting up in the sky.

Oliver Thaxter (6)
Ingoldisthorpe CEVA Primary School, King's Lynn

My First Acrostic – The East

Birds

B irds make nests
I saw a bird fly in the sky
R oaming birds
D arting, flying in the sky
S eagulls eat chips.

Angelina Robinson-Lagopodi (6)
Ingoldisthorpe CEVA Primary School, King's Lynn

Birds

B irds make nests
I n the sky
R obins have red chests
D ashing birds are nice
S ea is where they live.

Mollie Skerritt (5)
Ingoldisthorpe CEVA Primary School, King's Lynn

Dancing Birds

B irds fly high in the sky
I nto the cloudy sky
R e-nesting in the old tree
D ancing blue tits
S omething beautiful.

Olivia Hammond (7)
Ingoldisthorpe CEVA Primary School, King's Lynn

Birds

B lue tits can fly
I n the sky
R eally high
D ark nights
S omething will maybe get them.

Max Godwin (5)
Ingoldisthorpe CEVA Primary School, King's Lynn

My First Acrostic – The East

Me And My Family

M y name is Gabriella
E very day I go to school

A nd learn lots of things
N oon I have lunch
D o work hard says the teacher

M e and my friends play in the playground
Y oung is what we are

F riday is when I go swimming
A ll my family go too
M y mum showed me how to swim
I hope you can all swim
L uckily I have my family
Y ou should all be lucky too.

Gabriella Charlotte Oldham (7)
John Bramston Primary School, Ilford

Penny Farthing

P enny Farthing is a high-wheeled bicycle
E nables high speed
N ot very easy to direct
N ot very easy to go uphill, but
Y ou can ride it for novelty

F arthing is an old British coin
A re you aware of it?
R arely hoarded
T oo small to see
H elp me with a metal detector
I t is worth a quarter of a penny
N ow you can join Penny and Farthing
G o and enjoy the ride.

Ruth Sarah Chandy (5)
John Bramston Primary School, Ilford

Sun

S ummer days are full of fun
U nder the sun we play and run
N ever stay too long without sun cream on.

Erin Phippin (6)
John Bramston Primary School, Ilford

My First Acrostic – The East

Friendship

F riendship is nice
R especting everyone, helping and being kind to the people on the Earth
I love everyone that I know
E veryone needs to be kind
N ever fight in school
D reams are magical
S haring with friends is nice
H appy friends make me smile
I am a happy girl
P ennie is my friend.

Abbie Hazelden (5)
John Bramston Primary School, Ilford

Isobel

I sobel is lovely
S unshine Care Bear
O ctopus gets tentacles
B alls are black and white
E ating food is nice
L oving is pretty.

Isobel Jones (5)
John Bramston Primary School, Ilford

Lamborghini

L ook at this sporty car
A nd its colour shining bright
M aserati is his friend
B oth are zooming across the wet end
O il is burning fast when Ferrari's passing by
R oaring their engines loud
G ears shifting very fast
H ow about if all of them push the gas until the end?
I love watching this speedy car going through the bendy track
N oise is everywhere, like the banners in the air
I know Lamborghini is the winner – is simply the best!

Natalie Granese (7)
John Bramston Primary School, Ilford

Pirate

P olly is a parrot
I 'm captain of the ship
R un and hide from the bad pirates
A ship on its way
T he tide is high
E yes spy, they are on their way.

Luke Anthony McManus (6)
John Bramston Primary School, Ilford

Formula One

F astest and the best is Lewis Hamilton
O ne of the greatest sports
R ace is very interesting
M any countries went per season
U se the best of motor technology
L ots of people love this sport
A yrton Senna is the legend

O rganisations of Grand Prix has a high
N ames of drivers are written in history
E very driver is a brave man.

Matvejs Androsovs (6)
John Bramston Primary School, Ilford

Pirates

P irates are cruel
I am terrified of them
R iots they cause
A nd they take everything away
T reasure is a pirate's dream
E veryone is scared of pirates
S ee them coming and fight for your life.

Aisha Adebajo-Martinez (7)
John Bramston Primary School, Ilford

Jolly Roger

J umping, jostling pirates shouting
O verboard, overboard!
L aughing loudly at the
L and lovers
Y elling, 'Look out, look out!'

R oaring, ruthless pirates out on the
O cean waves
G old they seek
E verywhere
R eturning with their treasures.

Connor Joseph Cooper (7)
John Bramston Primary School, Ilford

Snowman

S nowmen like the cold
N ever sleep in the cold
O r else you will catch
W here is it snowing
M ountains are very cold
A way said the penguins
N odding to the igloo.

Ariane-Dannielle Forson (6)
John Bramston Primary School, Ilford

Gymnastics

G ymnastics is my favourite thing
Y es, I love it so much
M ats, benches and balance beams ready
N ow it's time to get going
A nyone can do it
S it ups and star jumps warm me up
T hen I am ready to do some vaults
I can do cartwheels and hand stands
C ount how many times I roll
S o at the end of my lesson I've got even better.

Nia Clairmont (6)
John Bramston Primary School, Ilford

Address

A ddress is very important
D o you know where you live?
D oor number tells you where to knock
R edbridge is a nice area
E veryone likes Chigwell
S chool is not too far away
S ometimes I love going there.

Kayah Roznicka (5)
John Bramston Primary School, Ilford

Vegetables

V eggies are so good
E at them every day
G reen ones, red ones, all different colours
E at them all up
T all ones, short ones, round and fat
A ll are yummy, put them in your tummy
B ake them, boil them, steam them
L ick your lips and say mmm
E njoy, enjoy, enjoy your veggies
S ave some for me!

Charlotte Ashton (5)
John Bramston Primary School, Ilford

Cheetah

C heetahs are fast
H ow fast can she go?
E yes search for prey
E ach step she silently moves
T eeth are sharp
A nimals are terrified to be near her
H unting over, hungry belly now full.

Amelie Parr (6)
John Bramston Primary School, Ilford

Swimming

S plashing
W et
I n the pool
M y favourite thing to do
M ucking around jumping
I n and out
N eed to remember my costume and
G oggles too.

Amy Branch (6)
John Bramston Primary School, Ilford

Scarlett

S is for sweet
C is for crazy
A is for amazing
R is for reliable
L is for lovely
E is for exciting
T is for terrific
T is for talented.

Scarlett Georgina Givens Hunter (6)
John Bramston Primary School, Ilford

Pancakes

P uffy and fluffy
A s golden as a coin
N ot for babies
C hocolate spread
A pancake as sweet as chocolate
K eep on eating until you're full
E xtremely sweet
S oft as a cushion.

Marley Stewart (6)
John Bramston Primary School, Ilford

Holidays

H ello Mr Holiday
O pen your arms wide for us
L ook after us all the way through
I n your cosy home we enjoy
D ay and night
A lways missing you and
Y our yellow beach
S ee you soon!

Krishna Seeburrun (6)
John Bramston Primary School, Ilford

My First Acrostic – The East

Dinosaur

D iplodocus herbivore,
I guanodon slow,
N igersaurus sauropod,
O viraptor speedy.
S altopus leaping,
A llosaurus carnivore,
U tahraptor vicious,
R ugops scavenger.

Kishan Shah (5)
John Bramston Primary School, Ilford

Parents

P eople who I love and care for
A re my mum and dad
R espect, admiration, I will always have for them
E ntire life
N obody will change their place
T hey are my rock and hope and definitely my
S uper parents.

Amelia Botnari (6)
John Bramston Primary School, Ilford

Monster

M onsters are stinky
O gres are slow
N obody likes monsters
S cary, weird and crazy
T errible and nasty
E veryone hide
R un quick, like Usain Bolt.

Riley Hunt (6)
John Bramston Primary School, Ilford

Arsenal

A rsenal, Arsenal, go! Go! Go!
R eady to play, Arsenal go
S ometimes will be first, sometimes not
E verybody shouts Arsenal! Arsenal!
N ever gives up
A lways be the star
L ondon, the best team is Arsenal.

Alan Oleksiewicz (7)
John Bramston Primary School, Ilford

My First Acrostic – The East

Numaya

N umaya likes chocolate
U nder my bed
M y mum loves me
A pples are my favourite fruit
Y ummy food my mum makes
A pril is my dad's birthday.

Numaya Polpitye (6)
John Bramston Primary School, Ilford

Sweets

S ugary sweets
W ithout chewing
E ven though she hates not chewing
E mpty packets, no more sweets
T o eat
S weets so scrumptious.

Gram Brazier (5)
John Bramston Primary School, Ilford

Summer

S unshine, sunshine, sunshine is here
U mbrellas can go back inside
M any flowers are growing
M ums are planning to go on holiday
E xcitement all around us
R oses are growing.

Daniel Owolabi (6)
John Bramston Primary School, Ilford

Summer

S un is bright and burning hot
U nder the water is cool and colourful
M ost people go to the beach
M any sandcastles are built
E veryone is happy
R unning after kites.

Sebastian Archire (7)
John Bramston Primary School, Ilford

My First Acrostic – The East

Pirate

P lease don't take my jewels
I worked hard for this ship
R oaming the seas effortlessly
A sking for trouble all the time
T reasure seekers, rascals
E veryone runs away at your sight.

Emma Chikov (7)
John Bramston Primary School, Ilford

Hannan

H annan is clever
A nd is good at spelling tests
N othing can stop me from football
N ot even my daddy
A ttitude is good
N obody agrees with that.

Hannan Ijaz (7)
John Bramston Primary School, Ilford

Summer

S un shining down on the ground
U nder the umbrella safe and sound
M y body is very, very hot
M aybe ice cream will make it stop
E venings are longer, oh it's great
R unning around staying up late.

Rebecca Seville
John Bramston Primary School, Ilford

Chloe

C heeky and cuddly
H elpful and happy
L ively and loving
O nly six and a half
E veryone's friend.

Chloe Lipscombe (6)
John Bramston Primary School, Ilford

My First Acrostic – The East

Mummy

My cute mummy
Ultra mummy
Magic mummy
My lovely mummy
Yippee! Mummy.

Parth Joshi (6)
John Bramston Primary School, Ilford

Daddy

Dads are fun to play with
And to have real good times
Doing up my laces and
Driving me places
You should have a daddy like mine.

Jayden Bahra (6)
John Bramston Primary School, Ilford

Frost

F reezing in the morning
R elax in the warmth
O h!
S o cold
T ime to wrap up.

Noah Demetriades (6)
John Bramston Primary School, Ilford

Eliza

E liza has blue eyes
L aughing all the time
I n class she loves to learn
Z apping around on her roller skates
A nna and Elsa from Frozen are her favourite.

Eliza Holder (7)
John Bramston Primary School, Ilford

Gram

G ram is my best friend
R acing with him is fun
A t school we play together
M y best friend forever.

Ramone Phillips (5)
John Bramston Primary School, Ilford

Milly

M is for manners, I use my manners at lunchtime
I is for interested, I'm interested in animals
L is for lovely, just like me!
L is for love, I love my mum and dad
Y is for younger, my younger brother and sister.

Milly Down
Littlegarth School, Colchester

Lauren Climpson

L is for lovely Lauren, I try my best to make people happy
A is for amazing Lauren, I try to make people amazing too
U is for under, Lauren is under the table
R is for running, Lauren likes running
E is for eggs, Lauren likes eggs
N is for numbers, Lauren likes numbers

C is for candles, candles are dangerous when they are lit
L is for Lori, my mum's name is Lori
I is for incredible, incredible is a nice word
M is for magic, magic is real
P is for penguin, they are my favourite animal
S is for star, Lauren is a star
O is for open, I can open the door
N is for naughty, sometimes I am naughty.

Lauren Valerie Climpson (6)
Littlegarth School, Colchester

My First Acrostic – The East

Isabella Grice

I is for ice cream that I really like
S is for shimmer, that is my pet
A is for alligator, who I happened to meet
B is for beautiful Isabella who is very pretty
E is for excellent school that I love
L is for laughter that I have with my friends
L is for Lyla my best friend
A is for athletes that I wish to meet some day

G is for gymnastics which I love
R is for rainbow that I love
I is for ice that I go skating on
C is for Chinese that I learn at school
E is for experiments that I like to do at home.

Isabella Grice (7)
Littlegarth School, Colchester

Jemima Howard

J is for jolly Jemima who is laughing all the time
E is for enjoying myself
M is for monkey, I am a cheeky monkey
I is for interested in endangered species
M is for mischievous Jemima who is very naughty
A is for amazing Jemima who does amazing things

H is for honey, I like the smell of it
O is for oranges, they are one of my favourite fruits
W is for wombat, I really like them
A is for afraid, I am afraid of the dark
R is for Rose, Rose is my middle name
D is for dove, Jemima means Dove.

Jemima Howard (6)
Littlegarth School, Colchester

Megan

M is for maths, maths is magnificent
E is for eating, my favourite food is roast dinner
G is for giggling, I giggle with my friends
A is for art, I like creating pretty pictures
N is for naughty, nobody's naughty!

Megan Palmer
Littlegarth School, Colchester

My First Acrostic – The East

Oliver Pashby

O is for ostrich my favourite animal
L is for lifeboat, I have a membership
I is for ice that is cold
V is for vegetable that I don't like
E is for elbows, I have two
R is for raspberry my favourite food

P is for pence because I get 500 pence every week
A is for Alfie, my pet rabbit
S is for shark, my favourite fish
H is for hungry because I am always hungry
B is for bells because my mum teaches music
Y is for yawn because I yawn a lot.

Oliver Pashby (6)
Littlegarth School, Colchester

Henry

H ungry, yummy Henry
E lephant Henry stomping around here
N ice Henry here today
R acing Henry, against my brother
Y ellow is my favourite colour.

Henry Rutland (5)
Littlegarth School, Colchester

Phoebe Racher

P is for panda, Phoebe a lovely animal
H is for holly, I love the smell
O is for otter, I love them
E is for even, I love even numbers, I am six
B is for brave, I am very brave
E is for eggs, I love Easter eggs

R is for rainbow, there are so many different colours
A is for alligator, they frighten me
C is for caterpillar, I like them because they turn into butterflies
H is for horse, they are very fast and soft, I love them
E is for Egypt, it is very hot
R is for raspberries, yum yum, I love them.

Phoebe Cecilia Racher (6)
Littlegarth School, Colchester

Henry

H is for helpful
E is for excellent
N is for nice
R is for right
Y is for yes!

Henry Staines
Littlegarth School, Colchester

My First Acrostic – The East

Monty

M is for Monty the monster
O is for outstanding Monty
N is for naughty
T is for tennis champion
Y is for young youngster

M is for Morgan
O is for old
R is for Romans
G is for great
A is for alligator
N is for nice Monty, also naughty.

Monty Morgan (7)
Littlegarth School, Colchester

Krisha

K is for kind just like me!
R is for run, I run fast
I is for ice cream, I love ice cream
S is for soft toys, I love soft toys
H is for hide, I am good at hiding
A is for apple, I like crunchy apples.

Krisha Donepudi
Littlegarth School, Colchester

Lyla Belshaw

L is for laughing, I love to laugh a lot
Y is for yawning, when I'm tired I yawn a lot
L is for loving, I love my family so much
A is for awesome gymnastics

B is for big brother, I have one
E is for exciting, sometimes I'm excited
L is for little, I have a little brother and sister
S is for smiling, I love to smile
H is for handstands, I love to do them
A is for amazing cartwheels
W is for wonderful art.

Lyla Belshaw (7)
Littlegarth School, Colchester

Winter

We are having fun
I like to ski
N ew Year is fun
T he snow is fluffy
E verywhere is snowy
R eally icy.

Isabella Windridge (5)
Littlegarth School, Colchester

My First Acrostic – The East

Harry Tucker

H is for hungry because I'm always hungry
A is for afternoon because I like the afternoon
R is for rely because people can rely on me
R is for rhythm because I can make rhythms
Y is for yellow sweetcorn that I really like

T is for talents because I have talents
U is for untidy because I'm not really tidy
C is for crocodile because I like crocodiles
K is for keyboard because I learn the keyboard
E is for exercise because I exercise every morning
R is for roast, my favourite food.

Harry Tucker (7)
Littlegarth School, Colchester

Isobel

I is for incredible Isobel
S uper-duper Isobel
O utstanding Issy
B is for blue, my favourite
E is for excellent Issy
L aughing Issy.

Isobel Sarah Christey (6)
Littlegarth School, Colchester

Archie Ball

A is for amazing rugby player
R is for running, I love running around
C is for caring, caring is good for people
H is for hyper, I am really hyper!
I is for ice cream, I love ice cream
E is for excellent Archie

B is for ball, I love to play football
A is for adorable Ella, my sister
L is for lovely Esme, my sister
L is for laughing, I'm always laughing.

Archie Ball (7)
Littlegarth School, Colchester

Otis Gee

O is for odd old Otis
T is for tickling Otis
I is for incredible, insane Otis
S is for silly, super Otis

Gee is for guitar-learning Otis
E is for escaping Otis
E is for Empire of Otis.

Otis Gee (6)
Littlegarth School, Colchester

My First Acrostic – The East

Henrietta

H is for happy every day, happy, happy Henrietta
E is for elephants, lovely for Henrietta
N is netball, fantastic and cool
R is for red, my favourite colour
I is for interesting things like lavender
E is for elephant
T is for thoughtful about my family and friends
T is for teacher, best ever teacher
A is for art and sport, cool!

Henrietta Stenning (7)
Littlegarth School, Colchester

Theodora

T is for terrific Theodora
H is for happy Theodora
E is for expert which I sometimes am
O is for outfit which I wear at school
D is for drawbridge
O is for order, I order my brother
R is for rattle, I had a rattle once
A is for art, I love art.

Theodora Langdon (7)
Littlegarth School, Colchester

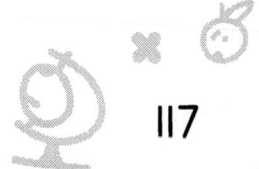

Imogen

I is for intelligent, I am intelligent at piano
M is for memory, I have a good memory to remember my school bag
O is for outstanding, I am outstanding at music
G is for graceful, I am graceful at dancing
E is for excellent, I am excellent at reading
N is for noise, I am loud.

Imogen Taylor
Littlegarth School, Colchester

Elliott

E is for exciting Elliott running all the time
L is for licking lollipops every time at the Indian restaurant
L is for lucky all the time
I is for ice cream, I love ice cream
O is for octopus, an octopus has eight legs
T is for the total when adding and counting
T is for trees, climbing them.

Elliott Sadler (7)
Littlegarth School, Colchester

My First Acrostic – The East

Samuel

S is for sport, I like football
A is for acting, I am good at acting
M is for maths, I am good at maths
U is for uniform, I have a blue uniform
E is for extraordinary
L is for leopard, I can run like a leopard.

Samuel Finan
Littlegarth School, Colchester

Hayden

H is for happy, I will make you happy
A is for acrobats, I can do a front roll
Y is for yelling, nobody is louder than me
D is for dangerous, beware of me!
E is for excellent, I am excellent at maths
N is for neat, look at my writing!

Hayden Abishai Swampillai (7)
Littlegarth School, Colchester

Winter

W indy and snowy
I ce skating in the park
N ights are long
T hundery storms
E aves are icy
R oasted nuts.

Tait Ferguson (6)
Littlegarth School, Colchester

Winter

W indy, looking out of the window
I t is cold
N o sun
T rucks get stuck
E verything is white
R unning feels crunchy.

Alexander Forshaw (5)
Littlegarth School, Colchester

My First Acrostic – The East

Winter

Wet glass
I ce skating on the pond
N o leaves, all bare
T ea is hot
E aster is coming
R oast nuts.

Tierney Clarke (6)
Littlegarth School, Colchester

Winter

Wind whistling
I ce skating in the park
N ights are freezing
T rees have snow on the top
E aster is coming
R abbits are out.

Poppy Down (5)
Littlegarth School, Colchester

Winter

White and icy
I cicles hang sharp
N ights are frosty
T he birds can't find food
E xtra icy
R eally cold.

Mika Quayyum (5)
Littlegarth School, Colchester

Winter

Windy nights
I cicles hanging down
N o leaves on the trees
T he warm fire moves
E xtra clothes
R ugby playing.

Angus Strathern (5)
Littlegarth School, Colchester

My First Acrostic – The East

Evelyn

E is for elegant, I am beautiful and graceful
V is for violet, I like the colour violet
E is for Egypt, I love learning about Egypt
L is for letter, I love writing lovely letters
Y is for yo-yo, I love playing with my yo-yo
N is for nature, I love nature.

Evelyn Cook (6)
Littlegarth School, Colchester

Samuel

S is for sport, I like football
A is for acting, I am a very good actor
M is for maths, I am a maths magician
U is for unknown, I like finding out about unknown stuff
E is for enjoy, I like everything!
L is for learning, I am good at English.

Samuel Barker
Littlegarth School, Colchester

Winter

We like skiing
I like snow
N ew Year is nice
T he snow is gone
E veryone likes snow
R obins like snow.

Henry John Wilmot Price (6)
Littlegarth School, Colchester

Winter

Windy days
I cy playgrounds hurt our knees
N ights are long
T he roads are icy
E aster comes soon
R abbits are hungry.

Theodore Bond Roberts (5)
Littlegarth School, Colchester

My First Acrostic – The East

Winter

White and frosty
I cy and colder
N o sun
T ough ice and water
E arth is asleep
R ed robin is bright in the snow.

Sebastian Brockman Booth (5)
Littlegarth School, Colchester

Winter

Wind blows the trees
I have fun in the snow
N ew Year is fun
T he snow is fluffy
E verybody had presents
R eally icy.

Tilly Sexton (6)
Littlegarth School, Colchester

Winter

White days
I cicles shining
N o sun
T rees are snowy
E arth is sleeping
R eally cold weather.

Angus Learmont-Adderley (5)
Littlegarth School, Colchester

Winter

Winter brings snow
I build a snowman
N ow we ice skate
T oes get cold
E veryone is chilly
R obins sing.

Matilda Oliver (5)
Littlegarth School, Colchester

My First Acrostic – The East

Winter

When it is icy and cold
I ce skating is fun
N ights get longer and the days get shorter
T he trees are dark
E ven the birds shiver
R iding a toboggan.

Charles Langdon (5)
Littlegarth School, Colchester

Winter

We like snow
I ce is slippery
N ow it is frosty
T rees are bare
E veryone is happy
R obins sing.

Lukas Karlsson (5)
Littlegarth School, Colchester

Winter

Windy nights
I cy days
N ights are quiet
T iny stars of ice
E xtra icicles
R abbits hibernate.

Adithi Thayur (6)
Littlegarth School, Colchester

Winter

Winter is cold
I like playing in the snow
N ow I am going to play
T he pond is icy
E verywhere is frosty
R abbits hiding in their burrows.

George Romer-Lee (6)
Littlegarth School, Colchester

My First Acrostic – The East

Isaac

I is for ice cream because I love ice cream
S is for sporty because I love sport
A is for apples because I love apples to crunch
A is for Ancient Egyptians because I'm learning about them
C is for caring because I care for my friends.

Isaac James Mott (7)
Littlegarth School, Colchester

Molly

M is for magnificent, I am magnificent at horse riding
O is for opportunity, a good chance to do something
L is for leaping, I'm good at leaping
L is for literacy, I like literacy
Y is for yo-yo, I'm good at yo-yoing.

Molly Talbot
Littlegarth School, Colchester

Toby

T is for Toby my very first name
O is for outstanding, I'm very outstanding at golf
B is for brilliant, I am brilliant at home
Y is for yellow, my favourite colour.

Toby Robert Paul Bryant (7)
Littlegarth School, Colchester

Snowflake

S ettles into the snow so beautifully
N ice and soft to touch
O h how wonderful it is
W ind and snowflakes make such a storm
F lutters around, so pretty to watch
L et the snow tickle on your face
A s soft as a pillow
K eeps on blowing around
E xtremely rare, only comes once in a while.

Emily Iszatt (7)
Roxwell CE Primary School, Chelmsford

My First Acrostic – The East

Charlie

C harlie
H appy
A nd
R eally funny
L ikes his dad
I s for Mum
E ats bananas.

Charlie Wilson (5)
Roxwell CE Primary School, Chelmsford

Thomas

T homas
H appy
O n a hill
M agnificent
A nd
S hiny.

Thomas Porter (5)
Roxwell CE Primary School, Chelmsford

Olivia

O livia is a big girl
L ovely
I 'm brave, I'm
V ery good
I nventive
A nd fun.

Olivia Maund (5)
Roxwell CE Primary School, Chelmsford

Frozen

F rozen, just like snow
R ound frozen land
O ver, while Olaf sings
Z ero, zero snowfall in the bed
E verybody likes snow in Frozen Land
N othing like snow.

Abigail Simpson (7)
Roxwell CE Primary School, Chelmsford

My First Acrostic – The East

Hayden

H e is a hero
A lways funny and
Y awns when tired
D reams in bed
E ats lollipops
N ext to his friends.

Hayden Thorneycroft (5)
Roxwell CE Primary School, Chelmsford

Reece

R eece is rich, he
E ats fish and chips, he
E asily works, likes
C hocolate and is an
E verton fan.

Reece Carter (6)
Roxwell CE Primary School, Chelmsford

Stars

S tars are magnificent, they
T winkle when the skies are black
A light the
R oads, so we can
S ee.

Mya Phillips (6)
Roxwell CE Primary School, Chelmsford

Aaron

A aron is funny
A nd likes
R acing his bike and eating
O ranges and
N ew clothes.

Aaron Maund (6)
Roxwell CE Primary School, Chelmsford

My First Acrostic – The East

Tilly

T illy is fabulous
I s nice and kind
L ovely
L ucky
Y et useful.

Matilda Drakeford (6)
Roxwell CE Primary School, Chelmsford

Sunny

S hiny, bright sun
U ntil autumn comes
N ow there's a dark
N ight and I
Y awn when I'm tired.

Lucy Scott (6)
Roxwell CE Primary School, Chelmsford

Kaiya

K aiya is
A wake, likes
I ce skating and eating
Y oghurt
A nd painting.

Kaiya Launchbury (5)
Roxwell CE Primary School, Chelmsford

Love

L ove can be easy when
O laf's around, because being
V ery loving makes it
E asy to be good.

Nuala Elsie Hedges (7)
Roxwell CE Primary School, Chelmsford

My First Acrostic – The East

Liam

L iam is lovely
I s a marshmallow lover
A jelly eater and
M aking dinosaurs.

Liam Wawman (6)
Roxwell CE Primary School, Chelmsford

Lola

L ola is kind and
O wns a dog and
L ikes animals
A nd goes on adventures.

Lola Lawrence (5)
Roxwell CE Primary School, Chelmsford

Elsa

E lsa is
L ovely and
S he makes fluffy snow
A lways forever likes fluffy snow.

Daisy Georgina Hedges (7)
Roxwell CE Primary School, Chelmsford

Luke

L uke is a lollipop
U nusual Luke
K icks footballs
E pic Luke.

Luke Carter (5)
Roxwell CE Primary School, Chelmsford

My First Acrostic – The East

Cat

C uddly as a cushion
A nd as soft as feathers
T errific as a tiger.

Scarlett Langley (5)
Roxwell CE Primary School, Chelmsford

The Birthday Platter

B for biscuits, very crunchy
I for ice cream, very icy
R for raspberry, very juicy
T for tomato, very mushy
H for hamburger, very spicy
D for doughnuts, very sweet
A for apple, very fresh
Y for yoghurt, very thick.

Gauravi Harish
Stukeley Meadows Primary School, Huntingdon

Young Writers Information

We hope you have enjoyed reading this book – and that you will continue to in the coming years.

If you're a young writer who enjoys reading and creative writing, or the parent of an enthusiastic poet or story writer, do visit our website **www.youngwriters.co.uk**. Here you will find free competitions, workshops and games, as well as recommended reads, a poetry glossary and our blog.

If you would like to order further copies of this book, or any of our other titles, then please give us a call or visit **www.youngwriters.co.uk**.

Young Writers,
Remus House,
Coltsfoot Drive,
Peterborough
PE2 9BF.
(01733) 890066 / 898110
info@youngwriters.co.uk